WHY YOU SHOULD NEVER BEAM DOWN IN A RED SHIRT

WHY YOU SHOULD NEVER BEAM DOWN IN A RED SHIRT

AND 749 MORE ANSWERS TO QUESTIONS ABOUT

STAR TREK

ROBERT W. BLY

HarperPerennial
A Division of HarperCollinsPublishers

HarperCollins books may be purchased for educational, business, or sales promotional use. For information, please write to: Special Markets Department, HarperCollins Publishers, Inc., 10 East 53rd Street, New York, New York 10022.

FIRST EDITION

Library of Congress Cataloging-in-Publication Data

Bly, Robert W.
    Why you should never beam down in a red shirt and 749 more answers to questions about Star Trek / by Robert W. Bly. — 1st ed.
        p.   cm.
    Includes bibliographical references.
    ISBN 0-06-273384-2
    1. Star Trek television programs—Miscellanea. 2. Star Trek films—Miscellanea.   I. Title.
PN1992.8.S74B58   1996
791.45'75'0973—dc20   96-13755

96 97 98 99 00 ❖/RRD 10 9 8 7 6 5 4 3 2 1

To the Trekkers

Contents

Acknowledgments

Thanks to the following Trekkers for significant contributions of questions and answers to this volume: John Maddux, Andrea Williams, Jani Fleet, David Jasicki, Jonathan Klein, Eric Feigenbaum, Sandy Scherger, Jessica Amos, Erik E. Post, and Pamela Record. I'm especially grateful to John Maddux for permission to reprint material from his manuscript for *Classic Star Trek Television: The Definitive Quiz Book,* his work in progress. If you sent me material and I didn't mention your name, please accept my apologies for the omission. It was purely accidental, I assure you.

Introduction

With three TV series on the air (first-run episodes of *Deep Space Nine* and *Star Trek: Voyager*, plus syndicated reruns of *The Next Generation*), the popularity of *Star Trek* is at an all-time high. Says *TV Guide*: "The *Star Trek* phenomenon just won't quit. After seven motion pictures and with a fourth TV series, it's going stronger than ever."

The book you hold in your hands is a companion volume to our first *Star Trek* book, *The Ultimate Unauthorized Star Trek Quiz Book*. As we noted in the introduction to the first volume, the original mission of the U.S.S. Enterprise was a five-year voyage — but *Star Trek* has gone way beyond that. The seven *Star Trek* movies, for example, have grossed more than half a billion dollars in box office revenues. *The Next Generation* TV show has, at times, been the highest rated weekly syndicated TV series in America. And more than 20 million viewers tune in weekly for new episodes of *Deep Space Nine* and *Star Trek Voyager*.

More than 100 *Star Trek* novels have been published and, according to *TV Guide* magazine, there are over 500 amateur and professional *Star Trek* fan publications. Sales of *Star Trek* merchandise have passed the one billion dollar mark.

Star Trek is hot. And with new movies, TV episodes, and bios proliferating, the body of

Star Trek lore is growing. This book is designed to test your knowledge. You can quiz yourself and your friends, or simply read and recall your favorite *Star Trek* moments. If you enjoy this volume, you may want to get the first. Enjoy!

I do have one favor to ask. If you find a mistake, or have additional information you think would enhance a third volume in the series, please share it with me. You will receive full credit, of course. Write:

Bob Bly
The Center for Technical Communication
22 E. Quackenbush Avenue
Dumont, NJ 07628

P.S. After publication of our first *Star Trek* book, we did "*Star Trek* Jeopardy" sessions at *Star Trek* conventions and bookstores nationwide. If this continues, I hope to see you there.

Why You Should Never Beam Down in a Red Shirt

1. What two methods are used to activate the Enterprise's turbo lift?

2. How many science labs are on the Enterprise?

3. What are the names of the Enterprise shuttlecrafts?

4. How many people can ride in a shuttlecraft?

5. How fast is the Enterprise traveling at warp 8?

6. On which deck is the hangar deck located?

7. Who designed the Enterprise's computer?

8. What is the serial number of the starship U.S.S. Yamato? Who is its captain?

9. What *Star Trek* actor played himself on *The Simpsons*?

10. Who was Sarek's first wife? second wife? third wife?

11. Who are Sybok's parents?

12. Name the Federation officers involved in the plot against the Federation in *Star Trek VI: The Undiscovered Country.*

13. In what cartoon strip is Captain Kirk denied a promotion because he hired an "alien" (Spock)?

14. Why did Patrick Stewart walk off the set of *Good Morning America* during an interview?

15. With whom does Stewart go scuba diving in his free time?

16. Which of the seven *Star Trek* movies had the highest gross earnings?

17. What character does Majel Barrett play in *Star Trek: The Next Generation*?

18. What actor plays Picard's nemesis Q?

19. On which TV drama did William Shatner play a police officer? Who played his partner? When did the show run?

20. For what true-story TV drama series did William Shatner serve as host and narrator?

21. Who co-authored William Shatner's autobiography?

22. In the proposed but never made series *Aliens in Wonder*, where did James Doohan, George Takei, and Walter Koenig work?

23. What *Star Trek* actor played a bad guy on the science fiction TV show *Babylon 5*?

24. How much of an advance did Nichelle Nichols get paid to write her *Star Trek* autobiography, *Beyond Uhura*?

25. Which *Star Trek* actor appeared in the motion picture *Gunfight at the OK Corral*?

26. What company put out a line of *Star Trek* greeting cards?

27. How much did Spock's prosthetic ear tips fetch at a Sotheby's auction?

28. Jonathan Frakes provides the voice of this character on the animated series *Gargoyles*.

29. How much money did *Star Trek: Generations* gross in its first three weeks at the box office?

30. What characteristics, according to actor William Shatner, make for a good starship captain? a) strong b) courageous c) stalwart d) romantic e) intelligent f) cute

31. What is the "Kirk Jerk"?

32. What languages does Picard speak fluently?

33. Who plays Captain Kathryn Janeway on *Star Trek: Voyager*?

34. On what date was Data discovered by the Tripoli crew? When did he graduate Star Fleet Academy?

35. In what year did the action on *Deep Space Nine* begin?

36. During what years did the Enterprise's original 5-year mission take place?

37. Who was the first doctor to serve aboard the Enterprise?

38. When was the episode "The Cage" first broadcast in its entirety?

39. How old was the Enterprise when it was destroyed in *Star Trek III*?

40. Gates McFadden, who plays Dr. Beverly Crusher in *The Next Generation*, was previously known by this name.

41. A frequent guest star on *Star Trek*, Diana Muldaur played this character on *L.A. Law*.

42. What is a "foolie"?

43. What *I Dream of Jeannie* actor played CPO Garrison in the *Star Trek* episode "The Menagerie"?

44. To what soap opera star is Jonathan Frakes married?

45. Barbara Eden's ex-husband, he played Kang in the *Star Trek* episode "Day of the Dove."

46. What guest role did Caesar Belli, child of famed attorney Melvin Belli, play on the episode "And the Children Shall Lead"?

47. What actress made her TV debut playing Miri?

48. Frank Gorshin was the Riddler on the *Batman* TV series and played what alien on *Star Trek?*

49. Who played Lorisa on the episode "That Which Survives"?

50. He was assistant to the producer on *Star Trek* and a co-producer of *Laverne and Shirley*.

51. Who played Jahn in the episode "Miri"?

52. What regular from *The Patty Duke Show* played a difficult bureaucrat who gave Captain Kirk headaches in "The Trouble with Tribbles"?

53. Which *Starsky and Hutch* regular played Makora in the *Star Trek* episode "The Apple"?

54. Who played Commodore Matthew Decker in "The Doomsday Machine"?

55. Who plays The Keeper in "The Menagerie"?

56. In what year was the first *Star Trek* movie made?

57. What is Troi's special power?

58. What illness did Sarek suffer from during the last years of his life?

59. What creature cared for and befriended Zefram Cochrane?

60. What happens to Wesley Crusher when he applies to Starfleet Academy?

61. What *Star Trek* actor guest starred on the short-lived Christopher Lloyd TV series *Deadly Games?*

62. Who was the first female Starfleet commander?

63. What position did Kathryn Janeway hold before being promoted to captain?

64. What does Captain Janeway do for relaxation?

65. On *Star Trek: Voyager,* with what enemies of the Federation does the Voyager crew join forces to find their way home?

66. What is the recommended Federation speed limit for starships? the maximum speed they can obtain under normal circumstances?

67. With how many lifeboat spacecraft is the Enterprise equipped? What is the maximum number of passengers a lifeboat can accommodate?

68. What is the "captain's yacht"? What does Picard name his yacht?

69. How long do you have to serve aboard a starship before you can redecorate your quarters?

70. On what deck is Sick Bay located?

71. What is the official name of Picard's starship in the movie *Generations?* How many starships were called Enterprise before it?

72. How do Picard's crew members access the ship's library for leisure reading?

73. Which Enterprise shuttlecraft is named after a Space Shuttle Challenger astronaut?

74. With how many tractor beam emitters is *The Next Generation's* Enterprise equipped?

75. How much wastewater and sewage is generated on the Enterprise each day per crew member?

76. How do you say "shut up" in Klingon?

77. What does the Klingon phrase "Dochvetlh vISoplaHbe" mean?

78. Why did First Officer Chakotay temporarily leave the Federation?

79. Who is communications officer aboard the *Voyager*?

80. Of what race is *Voyager* chief engineer B'Elanna Torres?

81. How old is Security Officer Tuvok?

82. What *Voyager* actor was a regular on the TV series *China Beach*?

83. What's the odd thing about Doc Zimmerman?

84. Who plays Neelix?

85. Members of what alien race have a lifespan of only nine Earth years?

86. What *Star Trek* actor says he once recorded a cartoon voice-over while he was in the bathroom?

87. How well did *Generations* do in the box office rankings during its debut weekend?

88. Bill Mumy, a regular on TV's *Lost in Space*, later became a regular in this science fiction series: (a) *Star Trek* (b) *Star Trek: The Next Generation* (c) *Star Trek: Deep Space Nine* (d) *Star Trek: Voyager* (e) *Babylon 5*

89. Who plays Kira on *Deep Space Nine*?

90. What *Star Trek* actor played Prospero in *The Tempest* on Broadway?

91. What college offered a two-semester course in *Star Trek*?

92. What musical instrument does William Riker play?

93. Who played Dr. Boyce in the first *Star Trek* pilot?

94. What *Voyager* actor played Billy Crystal's wife in *Throw Momma From the Train*?

95. Who designed the U.S.S. Voyager?

96. Who plays communications officer Harry Kim?

97. What injuries did Gene Roddenberry sustain in the crash of Pan Am Flight 121 from India to Turkey?

98. Patrick Stewart appears in this science fiction movie based on a classic SF novel by Frank Herbert.

99. Who plays the evil Soran in *Generations*?

100. From what planet does the Jewel of Thesia come?

1. James Kirk's middle initial is usually given as T. What other middle initial was used in at least one episode?

2. Which of the following commendations has Kirk received? (a) The Palm Leaf of Axanar Peace Mission (b) Grankite Order of Tactics (c) Class of Excellence (d) Prantares Ribbon of Commendation (e) Awards of Valor

3. Who is director of mining operations on Tyrus VIIA?

4. What is Spock's serial number?

5. What is Spock's blood pressure?

6. With what woman did Spock have a relationship before joining the crew of the Enterprise?

7. What is Dr. McCoy's medical specialty?

8. Where is Dr. McCoy's family from?

9. With whom did Mr. Scott fall in love in the episode "Who Mourns for Adonis"?

10. What was Sulu's original position on the Enterprise crew?

11. List four of Sulu's hobbies.

12. What is one of Lt. Uhura's artistic talents?

13. What career did Nurse Chapel give up to sign aboard the U.S.S. Enterprise?

14. To whom was Nurse Chapel once engaged before she had a crush on Mr. Spock?

15. To what Earth city did Chekov often compare "exceptional phenomena"?

16. What woman contributed to Chekov's "death" in the episode "Specter of the Gun"?

17. What was the room number of Yeoman Rand's quarters?

18. Why was Yeoman Rand "reassigned" away from the Enterprise?

19. What was Mr. DeSalle's function aboard the Enterprise?

20. What was Mr. Leslie's job on the Enterprise?

21. Where was Mr. Sing's duty station on the Enterprise?

22. Who was the science officer on the U.S.S. Constellation?

23. What was the highest ranking officer aboard the Enterprise in the episode, "The Deadly Years"?

24. Who was captain of the U.S.S. Excalibur?

25. Who was captain of the U.S.S. Exeter?

26. How old was Dr. Richard Daystrom when he made his duotronic break-through?

27. Which two *Star Trek* actresses had love affairs with Gene Roddenberry?

28. According to *TV Guide,* how much will Patrick Stewart be paid for the upcoming *Star Trek VIII* movie?

29. At its peak, what were the ratings for the original *Star Trek* in the late 60s?

30. How many episodes of the original *Star Trek* series were made?

31. When and where was the first *Star Trek* convention?

32. What year did Leonard Nimoy write his book *I Am Not Spock?*

33. On what TV show did William Shatner pretend to insult fans at a *Trek* convention? Where did he tell them to stop living?

34. What museum sponsored "Star Trek the Exhibition" in 1992?

35. In what time zone do Kirk and Picard go horseback riding together?

36. What does remodulation do to the deflectors?

37. When you are transported by the transporter, where is your unique molecular code stored?

38. What is a Heisenberg compensator?

39. Commander Ben Sisko was lieutenant commander of this star ship during the battle of Wolf 359.

40. Who owns the clothing store in the Promenade of the space station?

41. What Deep Space Nine crew member is the only known member of his species?

42. This device produces coffee, food, and other everyday items aboard Deep Space Nine.

43. What is a ramscoop?

44. This super-powered space being calls Earth "mind-numbingly dull."

45. Why does a gang of thugs from Klystron 4 attempt to kidnap Lieutenant Dax?

46. Which Deep Space Nine shuttle is named after an Earth river?

47. Name the leader of the alien delegation known as the Waddi.

48. He is the Grand Nagus.

49. What price do the Miradorn thieves ask Quark to pay for the golden egg?

50. This actor plays Commander Sisko's son, Jake.

51. What special power does Security Chief Odo possess?

52. Whose body did the symbiotic Trill inhabit before joining with Jadzia?

53. Where did Dr. Bashir get his medical degree?

54. Major Kira Neyrs is (a) a Vulcan (b) a Bajoran (c) a Cardassian (d) a Ferengi (e) a Borg

55. When was the first episode of *Star Trek: Deep Space Nine* broadcast?

56. What is unique about the wormhole where Deep Space Nine is stationed?

57. The producers of *Deep Space Nine* include (a) Gene Roddenberry (b) Dan Curtis (c) Rick Berman (d) Harve Bennett (e) Michael Piller

58. This *Deep Space Nine* actor was a regular on Benson.

59. This *Deep Space Nine* makeup artist is the daughter of the makeup artist who designed Spock's ears for the original Star Trek Series.

60. The Ferengi use this deadly weapon to kill their enemies in hand-to-hand combat.

61. The outer space equivalent of Sushi, the Ferengi consider this to be gourmet cuisine ... although you and I wouldn't touch it.

62. Jake Sisko's best friend is this Ferengi boy.

63. How old is the Trill, Dax?

64. This *Deep Space Nine* actress appeared with Angela Lansbury in the play *Gypsy.*

65. Name the Deep Space Nine crew member who served aboard the U.S.S. Rutledge under the command of Captain Benjamin Maxwell.

66. Which *Deep Space Nine* actor appeared in the movie *Star Trek VI: The Undiscovered Country*?

67. Avery Brooks, who plays Commander Benjamin Sisko, played Hawk to this actor's Spencer on the TV series *Spencer for Hire.*

68. Who created the virus that infects various crew members of Deep Space Nine?

69. This *Deep Space Nine* crew member is the son of wealthy parents.

70. What *Deep Space Nine* regular appeared in the Clive Barker movie *Hell Raiser III*?

71. How long does it take to make Armin Shimmerman up as the Ferengi Quark each day?

72. Who delivered Keiko O'Brien's baby?

73. Benjamin Sisko's wife and Jake's mother, she was killed by the Borg in a space battle.

74. Name the cast member from the original *Star Trek* TV series who played the voice of a computer in the first episode of *Deep Space Nine*.

75. He was the former Cardassian ambassador of Bajor.

76. This *Deep Space Nine* actor played a Palestinian in the TV mini-series *Big Battalions*.

77. Colm Meaney, who plays Miles O'Brien in both *Star Trek: The Next Generation* and *Deep Space Nine*, costarred with Hugh Grant in this 1995 film, a romantic comedy.

78. Name the Vulcan Captain under which Benjamin Sisko served in the war with the Borg.

79. Who edited the *Star Trek* fan magazine *Enterprise Incidents*?

80. Which Trek actor played Jesus in the 1961 movie *King of Kings*?

81. Who played the older, crippled Captain Pike in "The Menagerie"?

82. Who played the "drill thrall" Shahna in "Games of the Triskelion"?

83. Who said: "As science fiction, *Star Trek* isn't much. There's not a fresh idea in all 3 years of it put together"?

84. What is the LNFC?

85. On what date was Gene Roddenberry's star on the Hollywood Walk of Fame unveiled?

86. When did Universal Studios hold its "Star Trek Exhibit"?

87. What composer wrote the theme music for *The Next Generation*?

88. Name the space probe invented by Dr. Paul Stubbs to explore the Alpha System.

89. Who directed the *Star Trek* episode "The Tholian Web"?

90. Originally, Spock was to have a metal plate in his stomach. For what purpose?

91. What science fiction writer once described Spock as "a security blanket with sexual overtones"?

92. Who beat out DeForest Kelley for the lead in the movie *This Gun for Hire?*

93. What Trek actress played an African princess in the *Tarzan* TV series?

94. In what science fiction feature film did Walter Koenig star?

95. Who costarred with George Takei in the TV show "The House on K Street"?

96. What difficult test was Kirk the first and only Starfleet student to beat?

97. What was the budget for the *Star Trek: The Motion Picture?*

98. In what episode did producers cut corners by using a toy model of the Enterprise as a second star ship?

99. What company provided the special effects for *Star Trek II: The Wrath of Khan?*

100. What Trek actor directed Diane Keaton in the motion picture *The Good Mother?*

1. On what planet did Captain Kirk plan to strand the super-powered Gary Mitchell?

2. How cold did the surface of this planet get?

3. Where was the Enterprise heading at the beginning of the episode, "Tomorrow is Yesterday"?

4. Why was the planet Deneva colonized?

5. What quasar-like formation did the Enterprise encounter in the episode "The Galileo Seven"?

6. In what space quadrant was Trelane's planet located in the episode "The Squire of Gothos"?

7. What kind of colony did the Enterprise crew visit in the episode "This Side of Paradise"?

8. Where was the Enterprise headed when the first "winking out" phenomenon occurred?

9. In "Errand of Mercy," what planet became the focal point of fighting between the Federation and the Klingons?

10. On what planet did Kirk's brother Sam live?

11. What was the surface temperature of the ice planet on which Dr. Roger Korby conducted his research?

12. Where is Starbase 12?

13. On what planet does the Galileo land in the episode "The Galileo Seven"?

14. What star base was about to nova in the episode "All Our Yesterdays?"

15. Next to what star system was the planet Gamma Hydra IV located?

16. Who frequently says, "Hailing frequencies open"?

17. How many crew members served aboard the Enterprise during its original mission?

18. Who played Balok in "The Corbomite Maneuver"?

19. Who is the only female crew member to wear a mini-skirt?

20. Who is Quark's best customer?

21. On what planet was Tasha Yar born?

22. What *Star Trek* actor did *TV Guide* call "the most bodacious man on TV"?

23. What is the term for the Vulcan soul that can be transferred to another person at the time of death?

24. How do you say "Where is the bathroom?" in Klingon?

25. What does the Klingon saying "DaH ylDll qaStaHvlS wa' ram loS SaD Hugh FIjlah qetbogh loD" mean?

26. Which of these science fiction writers has written *Star Trek* books, movies, stories, or episodes? (a) Harry Harrison (b) Ray Bradbury (c) Roger Zelazny (d) James Blish (e) Harlan Ellison

27. What publication called *Star Trek* "perhaps the most enduring and all-embracing popular culture phenomenon of our time"?

28. In how many countries is *Star Trek* seen in its various incarnations?

29. What are annual gross sales for *Star Trek* merchandise?

30. How much have the seven *Star Trek* movies grossed at the box office?

31. In which *Star Trek* movie does Kirk die?

32. What is gagh?

33. On what date does the Enterprise investigate Pollux V in the Beta Geminorum system?

34. What world-famous theoretical physicist made a cameo appearance in *The Next Generation?*

35. How many Star Trek conventions are held annually worldwide?

36. How many copies of *Star Trek* novels and other *Star Trek*-related books are in print?

37. What *Next Generation* actor said of his audience: "If you go looking for geeks and nerds, you'll find some. But this is a show that is intelligent, literate, and filled with messages and morals — and that's what most of the people who watch are interested in"?

38. What is the prime directive?

39. What former writer of TV westerns said he envisioned *Star Trek* as a "*Wagon Train* to the stars"?

40. Who said, "The laws of *Star Trek* are totally fictional but are held by the fans with such reverence that they have to be followed as if they were Newton's"?

41. In *Generations*, how is Data able to experience emotions?

42. What is unusual about the bust of Gene Roddenberry in *Star Trek* producer Rick Berman's office?

43. What *Star Trek* actor was a member of the Royal Shakespeare Company?

44. How far in the future ahead of the original series does *Star Trek: The Next Generation* take place?

45. How is the Voyager transported to an uncharted region of the universe?

46. How was Kirk originally killed in the first studio version of *Generations?*

47. Translate from Klingon to English: bortaS blr jablu'DI'reH QaQqu'nay'.

48. What ship do the crew of Deep Space Nine use to travel through the worm hole?

49. Once "Bobby" on *Taxi*, he became part of the cast of the *Star Trek* look-alike series *Babylon 5*.

50. What characters are regulars on both *Next Generation* and *Deep Space Nine?*

51. What *Star Trek* actor appears in the movie *Timemaster?*

52. Siddig El Fadil recently changed his first name from Siddig to what?

53. What does Worf like to drink at bars?

54. Who wrote *Star Trek VIII?*

55. What happens to the Enterprise-D in *Star Trek VII?*

56. Where was the *Star Trek* convention "A Celebration of the Legacy of *Star Trek*" held?

57. What happened to William Shatner when he stood in back of an elephant during an African safari?

58. In what city did Kirk and Spock materialize after passing through the Guardian of Forever?

59. Iotians based their mob-ruled society on this Earth book accidentally left by the U.S.S. Horizon crew.

60. Where did the Godlike being Apollo live after leaving Earth?

61. On what planet is Scotty arrested for murder?

62. What planet is the Enterprise orbiting in the episode "Day of the Dove" when it encounters a Klingon ship?

63. Where does Kollos come from?

64. To what planet does the Enterprise travel in the episode "Wink of an Eye"?

65. Name the cloud city of Ardana.

66. What unusual biological properties does Lazarus possess?

67. What weapon do Talarian warships use?

68. Who is the captain of the Astral Queen?

69. Whom is Kirk accused of killing?

70. In what year did shuttlecraft Galileo crash on Taurus II?

71. What do the children in the episode "Miri" call adults?

72. Who killed Kyril Finn, the leader of the Ansata terrorists?

73. What position does Lt. Marla McGiver hold aboard the Enterprise?

74. What keyboard instrument does Trelane play?

75. Name the head of the High Council on Eminiar VII.

1. How many levels are there on a three-dimensional chess board?

2. How many slide levers are moved to energize the transporter?

3. Relative to other Star Fleet frequencies, what is special about the GSK 783 subspace frequency?

4. What does Code 710 mean?

5. In the episode "The Squire of Gothos," how does Kirk signal the Enterprise when his communicator does not function?

6. What kind of signal did Kahn's ship, the U.S.S. Botany Bay, send to the Enterprise when first encountered?

7. When the Enterprise goes back in time and is attacked by a U.S. fighter jet, what is the code name of the intercept jet?

8. On what space ship did James Kirk first serve?

9. How many ships like the Enterprise does Star Fleet have?

10. Who sponsored the United Federation of Planets creative and performing arts program?

11. What is the Elasian name for dilithium crystals?

12. How powerful is one ounce of anti-matter?

13. In the episode "All Our Yesterdays," what medium was used to store historical data?

14. In the episode "Empath," where did the creature draw the energy to power its force field?

15. What maneuver does the Enterprise use to defeat the Romulan vessel near Tau Ceti?

16. What kind of magic does Sylvia possess?

17. In the episode "Metamorphosis," what device did the Galileo crew use to communicate with the Companion?

18. What Vulcan soup does Nurse Chapel feed to Spock while he is in sick bay?

19. What was the Enterprise called in the parallel universe where an evil Kirk was its captain?

20. What is the magnitude of the sun of System Gamma 7A?

21. The UFO that crashed in the desert outside Roswell, New Mexico in 1947 contained which *Next Generation* characters, according to the show?

22. Who plays Jake Sisko as an adult?

23. With what Trill does Jadzia Dax have a same-sex affair?

24. What *Star Trek* actor appeared in the film *L.A. Story*?

25. How many years can Voyager travel without refueling?

26. At what speeds do the Enterprise and other starships of its class pollute the time–space continuum?

27. What year did Gene Roddenberry pass away?

28. To whom was Kate Mulgrew married in real life?

29. With what fellow *Star Trek* actor is Kate Mulgrew close personal friends?

30. In what TV show did Kate Mulgrew star during the late 70s?

31. How far from home is Voyager stranded?

32. First Officer Chakotay has a triangular marking over which eye?

33. What *Star Trek* actor appeared in the film *Eating Raoul*?

34. What sinister, multisect alien race is patterned after contemporary street gangs?

35. Neelix is from this race, whose world was destroyed by a nuclear bomb.

36. Why don't the Ocampa tend to get tan?

37. What is the Array?

38. What actor was beaten out by LeVar Burton for the role of Geordi, played a terrorist on *The Next Generation*, a Klingon mercenary on *Deep Space Nine,* and now plays Tuvok on *Voyager?*

39. The commander of Wesley Crusher's Starfleet squadron, he causes the death of a student during a gradua-tion-ceremony flight performance and then tries to cover it up.

40. Before he became Lieutenant Tom Paris aboard the Voyager, actor Robert Duncan McNeill was a regular in three TV series. Name them.

41. Who is Neelix's one-year-old girlfriend?

42. Is B'Elanna's father human or Klingon?

43. What *Star Trek* actor is married to *Voyager* casting director Eric Dawson?

44. What role did *Star Trek* actor Robert Picardo play in the TV series *The Wonder Years*?

45. What character does Jennifer Lien play? In what TV show did she previously star?

46. What *Star Trek* character consults his spirit guide in "vision quests" through the unconscious mind?

47. What is unique about Voyager's bioneural computer system?

48. Where did *Star Trek* producer Robert Justman "discover" Patrick Stewart?

49. Patrick Stewart wrote an hour-long TV play about Jesus Christ based on what novel?

50. What *Star Trek* actor played a bad guy on an episode of *Rawhide?*

51. With what planet was Eminiar VII at war?

52. Who was the leader of the Empire on planet 892–IV?

53. What destroyed System L–374?

54. What Enterprise crew member is killed by a Kligat thrown by a Capellan?

55. What did Spock find fascinating about Professor John Gill's approach to studying Earth history?

56. What rare psychological disorder can be caused by breakdown of neurochemical molecules during transporting?

57. How long before the Enterprise had the U.S.S. Horizon visited Iotia?

58. What actor provides the voice of M–5?

59. What is Carolyn Palamas's scientific specialty?

60. In the episode "All Our Yesterdays," what machine enables people to travel though time?

61. Why did all the adults on the planet Triacus commit suicide?

62. What metal alloy blocks transporter beams?

63. Who is the ruler of Yonada?

64. What device amplifies transporter signals to make beaming safer?

65. For how long had Bele been pursuing Loki when they ran into the Enterprise?

66. With whom does Scotty fall in love in the episode "The Lights of Zetar"?

67. When visiting a culture similar to Native Americans of 20th century Earth, with whom does Kirk fall in love?

68. What planet did Flint own?

69. Name the android Flint built for companionship.

70. Who is in charge of the installation on Elba II?

1. Name the three Organians present at the signing of the Treaty of Organia?

2. How old is the Metron who appeared when Kirk refused to kill the Gorn?

3. Name Dr. Adams' assistant at the Tantalus V penal colony.

4. What representative of the United Federation of Planets signed the Treaty of Peace with the Romulan Empire?

5. How old is Anton Karidian's daughter?

6. How old are the children in "Miri"?

7. What is the life span of a Harry Mudd android?

8. What is Sarek's official position?

9. In what year was Nomad launched?

10. What race built the Yonadan space ship?

11. How many lights appear on Yarnek's head as he talks?

12. Of what race is Marta, Consort of Lord Garth of Izar?

13. Who was the prosecutor of Argelius II?

14. What size is the giant protoplasmic creature the Enterprise encounters in space?

15. How much does Harry Mudd weigh?

16. What does the Klingon phrase "veQDuj 'oH DujlIj'e'" mean?

17. Where did Geordi's father study invertebrate biology?

18. What Cardassian tortures Picard in the episode "Chain of Command"?

19. What is t'hy'la?

20. What do the microbrains of Velara III call humans to insult them?

21. Where does Colonel Fellini of the 498th Air Base Group interrogate Kirk and Sulu when they accidentally travel back in time to Earth?

22. What device is implanted in the bodies of the people of Yonada to ensure that they follow the Oracle?

23. On what planet does McCoy's daughter go to school?

24. What computer rating does Spock hold?

25. What psychological test does McCoy give Kirk when his behavior changes after his body is taken over by the mind of his former girlfriend Janice Lester?

26. What is the "Vault of Tomorrow"?

27. What is a coalsack?

28. What substance cures the rapid aging certain crew members have undergone in the episode "The Deadly Years"?

29. Who is the alien entity to which Deanna Troi gives birth?

30. With what dressing or sauce is the Betazoid dish oskoid eaten?

31. What's wrong with the solition wave propulsion system invented by Dr. Jidar?

32. What type of whiskey are Chekhov, Spock, McCoy, and Kirk served at the bar when they are forced to act out the role of the Clanton gang in an Old West-style illusion?

33. What mineral is used in the life support systems of colony worlds in sealed biospheres?

34. What animal is the natural predator of the Tribble?

35. What vitamin supplement does Data feed to his cat?

36. What does the Vulcan term "kroykah" mean?

37. Which aliens attempt to take over Starfleet by getting Federation officers addicted to video games?

38. What is one of Geordi's favorite pasta dishes?

39. What comedian tries to teach Data to be funny?

40. What is the title of the science fiction novel written by George Takei?

41. In which of these TV shows has James Doohan *not* appeared? (a) *The Twilight Zone* (b) *The Mod Squad* (c) *Ben Casey* (d) *Peyton Place* (e) *Bonanza*

42. Again, in which of these TV shows has James Doohan *not* appeared? (a) *The Virginian* (b) *Then Came Bronson* (c) *The Immortal* (d) *Shenandoah* (e) *The Man from U.N.C.L.E.*

43. In what movie from a Tom Clancy novel did Gates McFadden appear?

44. Where were the original components for the Enterprise built?

45. Why shouldn't you touch the pod plants on Gamma Trianguli VI?

46. Which *Star Trek* actor's son played Boner on the TV series *Growing Pains*?

47. Why can't Salia, the future leader of Daled IV, go to the bathroom?

48. What radiation is emitted by subspace phase inverters?

49. When Kirk is engaged in a fight to the death with Spock on the planet Vulcan, with what drug does McCoy inject Kirk?

50. What machine do the Romulans use to extract information from their enemies?

1. How many crew members of the ensign grade were assigned aboard the Enterprise?

2. What color is the drink "tranya"? Romulan ale?

3. What episode of the original *Star Trek* is the only one in the series to hint at the existence of a rest room aboard the Enterprise?

4. What female officer wore a full dress uniform in the episode "Court Martial"?

5. What "medicine" does Dr. Boyce make for Captain Pike in "The Menagerie"?

6. This was the last episode in which Yeoman Rand appeared.

7. What poems does Spock recite when forced to speak aloud by Charlie X?

8. What song does Uhura sing in the episode "The Conscience of the King?"

9. What alien costume from a previous *Star Trek* episode can be seen in the alcove of Trelane's castle?

10. In which episode does Kirk accuse his crew of mutiny?

11. Who headed the first Federation science expedition to the Malurian star system?

12. What was the highest numbered star base ever mentioned in the original series?

13. In "Day of the Dove," for how long after the signing of the Treaty of Organia had the Federation and the Klingon Empire been at peace?

14. What insignia does Dr. Donal Cory wear on his uniform?

15. Which Bible verse does Dr. Ozaba quote in "The Empath"?

16. Who says, "Any home port the ship makes will be someone else's, not mine"?

17. Balok compares himself to this Robert Louis Stevenson character.

18. What was T'Prau's unique distinction in Federation political circles?

19. What creature on Antos IV can generate electrical shocks?

20. Who does Scotty drink under the table in the episode "By Any Other Name"?

21. What is the emblem of the Sciences Rank?

22. How fast is warp factor one in miles per second?

23. On what planet are researchers trying to develop a cure for the plasma plague?

24. On what planet does "The Conscience of the King" take place?

25. Spock wears the uniform he had on in "Spock's Brain" in only one other episode. Name it.

26. What medicine saves Kirk's life on the planet Neural?

27. What device does McCoy use to bring Kirk "back to life" in the episode "The Enterprise Incident"?

28. What medicine is used to treat Rigelian fever?

29. What disease strikes the inhabitants of Miri's planet?

30. What disease does Spock pretend to have to attempt to escape an alien prison?

31. Name the comic book series created by Leonard Nimoy.

32. With what drug does Dr. McCoy accidentally inject himself before leaping through the time portal that is "The Guardian of Forever"?

33. What stimulant did Dr. McCoy give Hanar?

34. What is a "harvester"? What can neutralize their effect?

35. Where is the Parada System located?

36. What kind of energy can prevent sensors and tricorders from functioning?

37. What beings have transparent skulls?

38. Why does Ensign Melora Pazlar need a wheelchair or crutches to walk when performing her duties aboard Deep Space Nine?

39. Where does Quark send his nephew Nog to steal ore samples?

40. What type of star is Wolf 359, the site of the Borg attack on a Federation armada? What are the Federation casualties in this battle?

41. What is Sisko's favorite Bajoran constellation?

42. How old is Jadzia? Dax?

43. What is Jake Sisko's favorite sport?

44. What artifacts dealer tries to add Data to his collection?

45. What disease causes Vulcans to release repressed emotions?

46. What being, after being rescued from an escape pod by the Enterprise, transforms into pure energy?

47. When Picard is temporarily turned into a Borg, what side of his face is given mechanical prosthetics?

48. With whose holodeck image does Geordi fall in love?

49. What are the Ullians?

50. Who develops the Exocomp, a problem-solving smart computer that can make repairs in areas of machinery that humans can't get into?

1. What happens during the "wink out" phenomenon?

2. Lazarus renders this female crew member unconscious.

3. Aliens destroy this planet in the episode "Arena."

4. Where did Kirk fight the Gorn?

5. The marriage of what two crew members never takes place because one is killed when the Romulans attack?

6. Why does the Romulan commander hesitate to destroy the Enterprise in "Balance of Terror"?

7. What is Charlie X's last name?

8. What flower does Charlie X give to Yeoman Rand?

9. In the "City on the Edge of Forever," who is the first crew member to require medical attention?

10. What had the Guardian of Forever been awaiting for billions of years?

11. What equipment does Spock steal from a church mission run by Edith Keiler?

12. What play do the Karidian players present?

13. What part of Dr. Leighton's body is disfigured by Kodos the Executioner?

14. What type of lubricant is used in the attempted poisoning of Lt. Riley?

15. What is the Enterprise's mission in the episode "The Corbomite Maneuver"?

16. What is the umbrella title of the series of science fiction novels written by William Shatner?

17. Who is the commodore of Starbase 11?

18. Name the members of the judiciary hearing Kirk's case in the episode "Court Martial."

19. What crew member accompanied Kirk to the Tantalus V penal colony?

20. What device on Tantalus V is used to control inmates' minds?

21. How many miners were killed by the Horta?

22. On what level of the mining planet did the Horta lay its silicon eggs?

23. What drink does the evil Kirk demand from McCoy in sick bay?

24. How did Spock discover his father's feelings for him?

25. Why did the Klingons want to take over Organia?

26. Who is the chairperson of the Council of the Elders on Organia?

27. What Federation dignitary is onboard the Enterprise in the episode "The Galileo Seven"?

28. What Galileo crew member is the first to die on Taurus II?

29. On what planet does archaeologist Nancy Crater conduct her research?

30. Whose identity does the salt vampire assume to get aboard the Enterprise?

31. Who was the first Enterprise officer to survive the salt vampire's attack?

32. How was Captain Pike exposed to the delta rays that caused his injuries?

33. Who is in command of the Enterprise when it leaves Starbase 11 in "The Menagerie"?

34. At maximum warp, how long does it take to go from Starbase 11 to Talos IV?

35. In the episode "Miri," the dying humanoid claims ownership of what children's toy?

36. What equipment does Dr. McCoy use to analyze viruses?

37. What were the names of Mudd's women?

38. What card game does the Mudd android Eve play?

39. What astronomical phenomenon did the Enterprise observe in the vicinity of Psi 2000?

40. In the episode "The Naked Time," how is the virus transmitted among Enterprise crew members?

41. What affliction affected various planets in the episode "Operation: Annihilate"?

42. What destroys the pancake-like creatures that have taken over Deneva?

43. What Federation ship disappears near the planet Beta III?

44. What device did Reger reveal to the landing party that was not consistent with the local culture in "The Return of the Archons"?

45. What life form did Mr. Rodriguez see during "Shore Leave" that, because sensors indicated the planet was lifeless, surprised him?

46. On shore leave, Teller is attacked by what jungle beast?

47. What were Kahn's first words upon being revived from suspended animation in the Botany Bay?

48. Who directed Leonard Nimoy in the recent remake of the *Outer Limits* episode "I Robot"?

49. What unusual space phenomenon does Spock detect near Trelane's planet?

50. What *Star Trek* actor appeared in a *Naked Gun* movie with O.J. Simpson and Leslie Nielsen?

51. Why did the Enterprise visit Eminiar VII?

52. How many casualties did Eminiar VII suffer per year in its interplanetary war?

53. How many colonists lived in the settlement Kirk visited in the episode "This Side of Paradise"?

54. Who wrote the *Twilight Zone* episode "Nightmare at 20,000 Feet" starring William Shatner?

55. What historic news event does the Enterprise crew hear about on the radio when they go back into Earth's past?

56. Name Captain Christopher's son.

57. Who is the "Louis Pasteur of archaeological medicine"?

58. Name the android created by the former inhabitants of Exo III.

59. What poem does Gary Mitchell recite to Dr. Dehner in sick bay?

60. What Trek actor once played a thug on the TV series *Get Smart*?

1. William Shatner has an avid interest in this hobby.

2. Who was the first security guard killed in the episode "The Apple"?

3. For what organizations did Gary Seven carry ID cards in his wallet?

4. Planet 892–IV has technological and industrial development roughly equivalent to Earth development of what century?

5. What stops ships from leaving the edge of the galaxy?

6. He is Sylvia's assistant and also a wizard.

7. How many inhabitants of the Malurian star system does Nomad destroy?

8. How old were Robert and Elaine Johnson in "The Deadly Years"?

9. For what solar system was the Doomsday Machine headed after destroying System L–374?

10. How many tribes are there on Capella?

11. How far had Kirk run when he asked Shahna to stop so he could rest?

12. How many "Alice" androids did Mudd create?

13. What word did android Alice 11B not understand?

14. What Federation ship has an all-Vulcan crew?

15. What issue was being considered at the inter-galactic conference at Babel?

16. What disease does Nancy Hedford contract on Epsilon Canaris III?

17. Who is the head spokesperson of the Halkan Council?

18. How many years passed between Kirk's two encounters with the deadly cloud creature?

19. What planet is at war with Ekos?

20. Who is captain of the starship Exeter?

21. What does McCoy accidentally leave behind on the planet Iotia?

22. Who is the leader of the Village People?

23. How far beneath the surface of the planet Arret do the three alien brains enclosed in spheres live?

24. What is quadrotriticale?

25. Who is the manager of the space station infested by tribbles?

26. What vessel did M–5 first destroy in "The Ultimate Computer"?

27. Apollo compares Kirk with these mythical Greek characters.

28. Who is the first murder victim in the episode "Wolf in the Fold"?

29. For what TV show did William Shatner write and direct the pilot episode?

30. What is the title of Nichelle Nichols' autobiography?

31. What actor, who played Dracula on Broadway and in a movie, did a guest spot on *Deep Space Nine*?

32. What fee does William Shatner charge to sign autographs at *Star Trek* conventions?

33. What former regular from *My Two Dads* stars as the hero on William Shatner's *TekWars* TV series?

34. What was the title of the first science fiction movie in which Leonard Nimoy appeared?

35. What was the name of the *Twilight Zone* episode in which William Shatner played a newlywed who stops at a diner on his honeymoon?

36. What *Addams Family* star played a giant android on a *Star Trek* episode?

37. William Marshall, who plays *Star Trek* computer genius Dr. Richard Daystrom, played what black vampire in the movies?

38. What was the "Tin Man" and what was unusual about it?

39. Why do Picard, Riker, and the rest of the Enterprise crew "lose" their memories of an entire 24-hour-period in their lives?

40. What space phenomenon can drive space travelers insane when their ship is traveling through it?

41. When *Newsweek* did a 1986 cover story on *Star Trek*, which character's picture was featured on the cover?

42. What super-powerful being traps the Enterprise in a void to experiment on the crew?

43. Name Data's creator.

44. Name Tasha Yar's sister.

45. What do the two-dimensional creatures who rob Troi of her powers attempt to do to the Enterprise and its crew?

46. Jean Simmons, who plays Starfleet Admiral Satie, played what character on the new *Dark Shadow* series?

47. What former *M*A*S*H* star plays Timicin, an alien scientist with whom Troi falls in love?

48. Who is arbiter of the Rite of Succession?

49. Name Worf's brother.

50. What Federation scientist wants to kill the crystal space entity to avenge her son's death on Omicron Theta?

1. What star system is about to nova in "All Our Yesterdays"?

2. Who is the head librarian on Sarpeidon?

3. Who is the leader of the scientific colony on Triacus?

4. What is prophesized on Triacus?

5. From where does the Enterprise hope to get zenite to transport to Merak II?

6. Who is the leader of the Zenite miners?

7. What lures the Enterprise to Beta XII–A?

8. How many Klingons die on board their ship in "Day of the Dove"?

9. Who tried to wrest the Tellun Star System from Federation control?

10. Who loves Elaan of Troyius (aside from Kirk)?

11. Who is Dr. Linke's research associate?

12. What aliens capture and then torture the Enterprise landing party to determine the qualities of humanoids?

13. In "The Enterprise Incident," how many Romulan ships surround the enterprise?

14. When Kirk disguises himself as a Romulan, what rank does he pretend to hold?

15. What disease nearly kills McCoy?

16. Who works with Miranda Jones?

17. What emotion does the blind Dr. Jones find distasteful?

18. What is stolen from Starbase 4?

19. Who is Chief Officer of the Commission of Political Traitors?

20. What cargo did the Enterprise deliver to Memory Alpha?

21. How many clairvoyant episodes does Lt. Romaine experience in "The Lights of Zatar"?

22. Why do the inhabitants of Gideon avoid contact with aliens?

23. Who beams down to Gideon to search for Kirk?

24. On what planet does the Enterprise crew discover a technologically advanced obelisk?

25. How fast is warp factor 2?

26. What gives the natives of Plato telekinetic powers?

27. How old is Sandra, wife of the leader of Plato?

28. Avery Brookes (Captain Sisko) portrayed what famous singer in a Broadway play about the life of that performer?

29. Where does the Enterprise travel for an antidote to the Rigelian fever affecting crew members?

30. Why did the Excalbians force the Enterprise landing party members to fight?

31. What weapon, popular on Vulcan and in Australia, do both Spock and Crocodile Dundee know how to use?

32. What is Uhura's native language?

33. As what Old West gang was the Enterprise landing party forced to act in the episode "Specter of the Gun"?

34. How long did Dr. McCoy have to retrieve and replace Spock's brain before Spock would die?

35. What did Kirk use to communicate with Spock's brain when it was removed from his body?

36. What is unusual about the earthquakes taking place on the planet the Enterprise orbits in the episode "That Which Survives"?

37. What starship is the Enterprise searching for when they run into the Tholians?

38. What happens to Chekov as a result of being aboard the Defiant?

39. Who is the Tholian commander?

40. Translate this phrase from Klingon to English: HaqwI' 'e' DaH yISam

41. Who is charged with taking care of Dr. Lester?

42. What spaceship was stolen by space hippies looking for the planet Eden?

43. How many inmates were on Elba II?

44. What enables the Scalosians to appear invisible and take over the Enterprise?

45. Who is Julie Nimoy?

46. What actress was originally slated to play Voyager Captain Janeway?

47. On what TV series was Robert Beltran a regular prior to *Voyager?*

48. What soap opera was Robert Duncan McNeill on before *Voyager?*

49. Air Force sorties routinely fly over this *Star Trek* actor's England home.

50. Why did William Shatner wear panty hose when doing horse-riding scenes during the filming of *Star Trek: Generations?*

1. Which episode of the original *Star Trek* took place over the longest period of time?

2. What Southern drink does McCoy enjoy?

3. What beverage does Balok serve Kirk and Bailey?

4. To what famous story does McCoy compare the bizarre "Shore Leave" planet?

5. What is the only episode of *Star Trek* in which the Federation is at war?

6. What nickname did Sulu give his favorite plant?

7. Lethe is treated by Dr. Tristan Adams. To what mythological river does her name refer?

8. In the episode "Conscience of the King," what type of drink does McCoy have?

9. What musical instrument does Uhura play?

10. What Irish song can be heard in the background while Kirk and Finnegan have a fistfight?

11. Captain Kirk called McCoy "Bones." What did McCoy occasionally call Kirk?

12. What is the Law of Argelius, according to Prefect Jarvis?

13. What does Hodin say is the only effective tool of diplomacy?

14. In what episode did Nurse Chapel finally kiss Spock?

15. When Kirk was forced to act out a role as part of the Clanton Gang, what newspaper did he read to keep up with events in the scenario?

16. Which of Garth of Izar's exploits were required reading at Starfleet Academy?

17. Who is recognized as the worst patient aboard the Enterprise?

18. The transporter was used for what unusual procedure in the episode "Day of the Dove"?

19. In what episode were most of the guest stars twins?

20. What was the name of the 1967 Halloween episode?

21. How many stripes does a commander wear on his or her sleeve?

22. How many stripes does a captain wear on his or her sleeve?

23. What instrument does Spock play?

24. What is the name of the tunnel-like tube providing the engineering crew access to the machinery of the Enterprise?

25. What is the technical name for the main viewing screen on the Enterprise bridge?

26. What is General Order 24?

27. What happens when living animal tissue is exposed to Berthold rays?

28. What does Code Factor One mean?

29. When Christopher Pike lost the ability to speak, how did he signal "yes" and "no" in response to questions?

30. When Starfleet Command issues an Automatic All Points Relay on Code One, what does it indicate?

31. What is a Class M planet?

32. What is the name of the military training institution for the United Federation of Planets?

33. What is the armed peace-keeping authority of the United Federation of Planets?

34. How can the Enterprise tow other space vessels?

35. What procedure must be followed when a starship's chief medical officer has a "reasonable doubt" about a crew member's ability to perform his or her duty?

36. What Star Fleet command order prohibits any Federation starship from visiting planet Talos IV?

37. The sonic disrupters used by the Eminians in "A Taste of Armageddon" are used as what other props in other *Star Trek* episodes?

38. How long is the final countdown once the Enterprise self-destruct sequence orders have been initiated?

39. What is a "Herbert"?

40. What substance contaminates the ryetalyn collected by M–4 in the episode "Requiem for Methuselah"?

41. How high above the planet Excalbia does the Enterprise orbit?

42. What element was needed to stop the plague on Merak II?

43. What colors were the filter elements in the filter masks Kirk offers the Troglytes?

44. At what meeting did Kirk tell Lt. D'Amato his geological report would startle people?

45. In the episode "Whom Gods Destroy," what security code words are used between Captain Kirk and Mr. Scott?

46. What machine gives Korob and Sylvia their powers?

47. What weapons do the Capellans wield?

48. What is a Dyson sphere?

49. What animal on Regulu V goes through a mating cycle similar to the Vulcan *pon farr*?

50. In the evil parallel universe, what instrument does Mr. Spock use to punish Mr. Kyle ?

51. What is Harry Mudd's full name?

52. What type of creature is a gorn?

53. Who is Dr. Roger Korby's male assistant?

54. What two Beta III residents provide assistance to the Enterprise shore party in the episode "Return of the Archons"?

55. Why does Hacom tell the Enterprise landing party members to leave Beta III?

56. Name Anton Karidian's daughter.

57. What experimental mining technique at planet Tyrus VIIA uses a force field to dig for mineral deposits?

58. Who accidentally destroys himself with Dr. McCoy's hand phaser when McCoy is sent back in time by the Guardian of Forever?

59. How many female crew members were aboard the Botany Bay?

60. What is the official title for the leader of the Talosians?

61. What materials were used in the skin and skeletons of Mudd's androids?

62. Who is the commander of the Klingon ship into which Kirk beams hundreds of tribbles?

63. Thelev, disguised as an Andorian, is really a member of what race?

64. The males of what race have luminescent silver-blue stars on their foreheads?

65. Who are the masters of the planet Triskelion?

66. How does the cloud creature reproduce?

67. Who is the ruler of the Utopian planet modeled after Plato's Republic?

68. What color skin do Troyians have?

69. What do Spock's mother and Batman's sidekick Robin have in common?

70. What alien rock creature forces the Enterprise landing party to fight facsimiles of historical figures from their native planets?

71. Where had Dr. Janice Lester been doing research before beaming aboard the Enterprise and attempting to take over Kirk's body?

72. What do the Preservers do?

73. Name the Medusan ambassador.

74. What did the men and women on the sixth planet of the Sigma Draconis system call themselves?

75. Name the tall, bald master of the drill thralls.

76. Who did Kirk discover aboard the Enterprise in the episode "The Mark of Gideon"?

77. Name the head of the Gideon Council.

78. What two spacecraft merge to form Nomad?

79. In the evil alternate universe, who saves Kirk from Chekov's assasination attempt?

80. What extra appendages does Akuta have on his body?

81. What industry is located on the planet Delta Vega?

82. Name the ambassador from the planet Troyius.

83. What class of starship has a sphere instead of a saucer as its primary hull?

84. What planet is dominated by women?

85. What mildly toxic plant grows on planet M–113?

86. The Enterprise crew finds creatures made of brain cells on this planet.

87. Where did Dr. Roger Korby conduct his research?

88. On what Starbase did Kirk stand trial by court martial?

89. What substance is mined on the planet Janus VI?

90. Where was the Enterprise headed when Trelane captured it?

91. Who is the wife of Prefect Jaris of the planet Argelius II?

92. What lethal nerve gas do Klingons sometimes use as a weapon?

93. In "The Menagerie," with whom does Captain Pike go on a picnic?

94. What is the chief industrial operation on the planet Rigel 12?

95. In what star system are the planets Elas and Troyius located?

96. What Earth observation outposts are destroyed in the episode "Balance of Terror?"

97. Where does Dr. Thomas Leighton live?

98. In what region of the galaxy is the "Shore Leave" planet located?

99. To what destination was the Enterprise taking the Karidian Players?

100. How many colonists originally settled the planet Omicron Ceti III?

1. What *Star Trek* actor does voice-overs for Saab commercials?

2. What *Star Trek* actor appeared in the Broadway play *The World of Suzie Wong*?

3. What heinous crime did Kirk commit in Harlan Ellison's unsold treatment for the first *Star Trek* feature film?

4. What *Star Trek* actor called his movie career "just plain ugly"?

5. What actor was the first choice to play Sybok in *Star Trek V*?

6. What *Star Trek* actor was a regular on the TV series *Here Comes the Bride*?

7. Translate the following phrase from Klingon into English: batlh Daqawlu'taH.

8. What is the Klingon equivalent of Kirk's favorite phrase, "Beam me up!"?

9. Who wrote the *Star Trek* novel *Masks*?

10. In what *Star Trek* novel is Riker captured by cave people protesting the destruction of their planet?

11. What is the Boogeyman?

12. In what *Star Trek* novel do fundamentalists leave Earth and form a government under which — as in Ray Bradbury's classic science fiction novel *Fahrenheit 451* — fiction is outlawed?

13. What *Star Trek* planet is named after *Star Trek* author Kevin Ryan?

14. In what *Star Trek* novel is Picard accused of treason and sentenced to execution by torture?

15. What are the Ferengi Rules of Acquisition and how many of them are there?

16. Who is the Grand Magus of the Ferengi?

17. What do the Ferengi say one should never let stand in the way of opportunity?

18. What is the Ferengi formula for business success?

19. Earth natives say "Anything worth doing is worth doing well." What do the Ferengi say about "anything worth doing"?

20. What is the Ferengi prescription for being a successful liar?

21. Out of what insect do the Ferengi make snuff?

22. What do the Ferengi say about dignity?

23. What is the Ferengi term for sexual intercourse?

24. What Cardassian is a tailor running a clothing shop on the *Deep Space Nine* space station?

25. What do the Ferengi do with the bodies of their dead?

26. Who plays Lt. Valeris, the Vulcan crew member who betrays the Federation in *Star Trek VI: The Undiscovered Country*?

27. What *Star Trek* actor carries magnetic business cards with his character's name on them?

28. Who is the shape shifter who double-crosses Kirk and McCoy in *Star Trek VI: The Undiscovered Country*?

29. What song do Kirk, McCoy, and Spock sing while sitting around a campfire?

30. What Charles Dickens novel does Spock give Kirk for his birthday?

31. What actress had her head shaved to play an alien in the first *Star Trek* feature film?

32. What star is at the center of the Malurian System?

33. What former *Night Court* star plays the Klingon Maltz in *Star Trek: The Search for Spock*?

34. On what Klingon ship does Riker temporarily serve? Who is its captain?

35. What is unusual about the planet Pacifica?

36. Name the Vulcan science officer who dies in a horrible transporter accident in the first *Star Trek* feature film.

37. What kind of force field is used to keep prisoners from escaping Klingon brigs?

38. What is the vitalizer beam?

39. On what planet are marriages considered unsuccessful if children are not produced within one year?

40. What is the real name of the entity that once possessed Jack the Ripper on Earth?

41. What creature drains the energy from the Gamma 7-A System, killing all living beings in the system?

42. To what institution does Dr. Theodore Haskins belong?

43. What regular from the TV series *Falcon Crest* played the helmsman of the U.S.S. Saratoga on *Star Trek IV: The Voyage Home*?

44. What area of space is loosely governed by tiny, childlike inhabitants of enormous starships?

45. Why do space travelers avoid visiting the planet Kzinti?

46. Isak, captured by the Ekosians SS, was an agent for what race?

47. How much did it cost to make *Star Trek: The Motion Picture*?

48. What *Star Trek* actress do Trekkers call the "Auntie Mame of the Galaxy"?

49. Name the actress who played Sovereign Marouk on *Star Trek* and the co-owner of the motel in the movie *Motel Hell?*

50. What former member of the singing group The Mamas and The Papas played Jenice Manheim, Picard's first love interest?

51. What subcontractor developed the docking port system for the Enterprise? When was it first used?

52. How long did it take the original Enterprise to accelerate from warp factor 1 to warp factor 4?

53. How long are the Enterprise's nacelles?

54. What spacecraft, smaller than the shuttles, are used by Enterprise engineering and maintenance staff to do exterior repairs to the ship in outer space?

55. How many photon torpedoes does the Enterprise carry?

56. What makes some Klingon vegetables blue?

57. What is the Klingon's home world?

58. What is a Gin'tak?

59. What historic figure do the Klingons hold in reverence?

60. Klingons eat the meat of this creature, which is considered a sentient life form by the Federation, tastes like lamb, and is cooked with the leaves and roots of the Toragh plant.

61. Which person affiliated with *Star Trek* once said: "I am a storyteller who has gotten a bit tired of having to always tell my stories through directors, actors, and studio policy decisions"?

62. Name the Jungian scholar who wrote the book, *Meaning in Star Trek*.

63. What *Star Trek* actor appeared in the play *Equus* on Broadway?

64. Where did Scotty live as a child?

65. Where was Sulu born?

66. Who was Chekov's first love?

67. Which crew member of the original Enterprise was a genetically engineered humanoid from the planet Larmia VI?

68. What did Nomad do to Uhura when she laughed at his request to explain the concept of music to him?

69. What did Dr. McCoy's father do for a living and where did he work?

70. What is a kahs-wan?

71. Name Kirk's parents.

72. For what are the Zakdorns famous?

73. When an alien probe makes Picard believe he is living an alternate life in which he did not join Starfleet, what does he imagine his profession to be? His hobby?

74. This prison escapee from penal colony Lunar V was programmed to be a master soldier when Angosia was at war.

75. What *Star Trek* actor directs in the fine arts program at Rutgers University in New Jersey?

76. Former *Hill Street Blues* actor Barbara Basson guest starred as what character on *Deep Space Nine*?

77. What Bajoran farmer, played by Brian Keith, refuses to leave his home in the episode "Progress"?

78. What *Star Trek* actor was quoted in *TV Guide* as saying: "The producers admit being very foolish and very lax in the way they've used me, or not used me"?

79. Where did Dr. Beverly Crusher have her private practice before joining the crew of the Enterprise-D?

80. How old is Guinan?

81. Worf's parents were supposed to have been killed in a Romulan attack on what planet?

82. What did Geordi LaForge's father do for a living?

83. What Enterprise-D crew member is Holder of the Sacred Chalice of Riix?

84. The crew of what starship discovered Data on the planet Omicron Theta?

85. Name Riker's parents.

86. When and where was Picard born?

87. Where did Sisko temporarily accept duty supervising the assembly of starships?

88. Name the Bajoran underground with which Kira once fought.

89. From what educational institution did Miles O'Brien turn down a scholarship to join Starfleet academy?

90. On what planet were Julian Bashir and his father stranded by an ionic storm?

91. What was Toban Dax's technical specialty?

92. What Deep Space Nine crew member spends part of every day as an amorphous blob of protoplasm resting in a tub?

93. What was Lieutenant Saavik's ancestry?

94. Who is murdered by assassins in *Star Trek VI: The Undiscovered Country?* What color is his blood?

95. In what unusual container do Betazoids deliver gifts?

96. In what species do sets of twins have a symbiotic relationship where the two halves make a whole person?

97. What is seloh?

98. What device can open hatch doors in emergencies by bypassing the normal door actuation servos?

99. What device does LaForge invent to help detect cloaked Klingon and Romulan ships?

100. What metal ingots are used as a medium of exchange outside the Federation?

Level I: Starbase Command

1. By a hand control and voice activation

2. 14

3. Galileo and Columbus

4. Seven

5. 512 times the speed of light

6. Level 19

7. Dr. Richard Daystrom

8. NCC 1305 E. Captain Donald Varley

9. Leonard Nimoy

10. T'Rea; Amanda; Perrin

11. Sarek and T'Rea

12. Colonel West, Admiral Cartwright, Lieutenant Valeris

13. Dave

14. He was offended because the weatherman was wearing a Starfleet uniform.

15. Brent Spiner

16. *Star Trek IV*, with more than $109 million

17. Laxwana Troi

18. John DeLancie

19. T.J. Hooker; Adrian Zmed; 1982 – 1987

20. *Rescue 911*

21. Chris Kreski

22. An outer space nightclub

23. Walter Koenig

24. $450,000

25. DeForest Kelley

26. Hallmark

27. $1,100

28. Xanatol

29. $57.6 million

30. a, b, c, d, e, f

31. His ship slingshots back in time

32. English, French, Klingon

33. Kate Mulgrew

34. 2338, 2345

35. 2370

36. 2264 – 2269

37. Sarah April

38. 12/93

39. 40 years old

40. Cheryl McFadden

41. Rosalin Shays

42. A game, trick, or prank played on an adult by a child

43. Adam Hayden Roark

44. Genie Francis

45. Michael Ansara

46. Steve O'Connell

47. Kim Darby

48. Bele

49. Lee Merriwether

50. Edward K. Milkis

51. Michael J. Pollard

52. William Schallert

53. David Soul

54. William Windom

55. Meg Wyllie

56. 1979

57. She is an empath.

58. Bendii syndrome

59. The Companion

60. He was rejected the first time he applied

61. Leonard Nimoy

62. Captain Rachel Garrett

63. Science officer

64. She "reads" holo novels

65. Maquis

66. Warp factor 5; warp 9.9

67. 400; 6

68. A multipurpose spacecraft for trans- porting visiting dignitaries to and from the Enterprise; Calypso

69. Six months or more

70. Deck 12

71. Enterprise-D; four

72. A personal holographic viewer

73. The Onizuka

74. Eight

75. 52 liters

76. bljath 'e' yimer

77. "I can't eat that"

78. He didn't agree with its ideals

79. Lieutenant Tom Paris

80. Half Klingon, half human

81. 150 years old

82. Robert Picardo

83. He is a hologram

84. Ethan Phillips

85. Ocampa

86. William Shatner

87. Number one, grossing $23.5 million

88. e

89. Nana Visitor

90. Patrick Stewart

91. Evergreen State College, Washington state

92. Trombone

93. John Hoyt

94. Kate Mulgrew

95. Rick Sternbach

96. Garrett Wang

97. Two broken ribs

98. Dune

99. Malcom McDowell

100. Streleb

Level II: Thrusters

1. R

2. a, b, c, d, e

3. Dr. Farralon

4. S 179 276 SP

5. Nearly nonexistent — cannot be measured

6. Leila Kalmoi

7. Deep space psychology

8. The southern United States

9. Carolyn Palamas

10. Astro sciences director and physicist

11. Botany, fencing, and collecting time-pieces and antiques

12. Singing

13. Biological research

14. Dr. Richard Korby

15. Leningrad

16. Sylvia, the dance hall girl

17. 3C – 46

18. The producers felt her romantic interest with Kirk would complicate scripts

19. He was a jack-of-all-trades

20. Navigator

21. Auxiliary control

22. Masada

23. Commodore Stocker

24. Captain Harris

25. Ronald Tracey

26. 24 years old

27. Nichelle Nichols, Majel Barrett

28. $5 million

29. It ranked only #52 in the ratings

30. 79

31. New York City, February, 1972

32. 1976

33. *Saturday Night Live*; he tells them "move out of your parents' basement"

34. The National Air and Space Museum

35. Nexxus

36. It boosts its strength

37. A pattern buffer

38. A device enabling the transporter to adjust to accommodate for the uncertainty of the speed and direction of the particles being transported

39. U.S.S. Saratoga

40. Garek, a Cardassian

41. Security Chief Odo

42. A replicator

43. A propulsion system that converts space matter into fuel for the spaceship

44. Q

45. They accuse Dax of treason and murder

46. The Rio Grande

47. Fallow

48. Zek

49. 1,000 bars of gold-pressed platinum

50. Cirroc Lofton

51. He can change into any shape or form at will.

52. Curzon Dax, Sisko's mentor

53. Starfleet Medical Academy

54. b

55. January, 1993

56. It is the first fixed, stationary wormhole ever discovered.

57. c, e

58. Rene Auberjonois

59. Janna Phillips, daughter of Fred Phillips, the first *Star Trek* makeup artist

60. Electronic whips

61. Live food of any kind, especially grubs

62. Nog

63. 300 years old

64. Nana Visitor, who plays Major Kira Neyrs

65. Miles O'Brien

66. Rene Auberjonois played Colonel West in this *Star Trek* film

67. Robert Urich

68. Dekon Elig

69. Julian Bashir

70. Terry Farrell, who plays Jadzia Dax

71. Approximately 3 hours

72. Lieutenant Worf from *Star Trek: The Next Generation* served as midwife

73. Jennifer Sisko

74. Majel Barrett

75. Gul Dukat

76. Siddig El Fadil, who plays Dr. Bashir

77. "The Man Who Went Up a Hill and Came Down a Mountain"

78. Storil

79. James Hise

80. Jeffrey Hunter

81. Sean Kenney

82. Angelique Pettyjohn

83. Science fiction writer Fred Pohl

84. Leonard Nimoy Fan Club

85. 9/4/85

86. 6/9/88

87. Dennis McCarthy

88. The Egg

89. Ralph Senesky

90. To consume energy to sustain him

91. Isaac Asimov

92. Alan Ladd

93. Nichelle Nichols

94. *Moontrap*

95. Dean Jaeger

96. Kobayashi Maru

97. $15 million

98. "The Doomsday Machine"

99. Industrial Light & Magic

100. Leonard Nimoy

Level III: Impulse Power

1. Delta Vega

2. −120° F

3. Starbase 9

4. It was to become a base for a freight line

5. Murasaki 312

6. Quadrant 904

7. Agricultural colony

8. Starbase 200

9. Organia

10. Deneva

11. −100° F

12. In the Gamma 400 star system

13. Taurus II

14. Beta Niobe

15. The Romulan Star System

16. Uhura

17. 500

18. Clint Howard

19. Deanna Troi

20. Morn

21. Turkana IV

22. Patrick Stewart

23. Katra

24. nuqDaq 'oH puchpa" e'

25. "4,000 throats may be cut in one night by a running man"

26. d, e

27. *Time* magazine

28. 75

29. $1 billion

30. Half a billion dollars

31. *Generations*

32. A worm that is a Klingon delicacy

33. Stardate 3468

34. Stephen Hawking

35. Approximately 200

36. 63 million

37. Jonathan Frakes

38. Never interfere with the development of any alien civilization or culture

39. Gene Roddenberry

40. Rick Berman, producer

41. An emotion chip is implanted in his brain

42. It is blindfolded

43. Patrick Stewart

44. 80 years

45. A space–time anomaly

46. Shot in the back with a phaser

47. "Revenge is a dish best served cold"

48. The Defiant

49. Jeff Conaway

50. Mr. and Mrs. Miles O'Brien, Worf, Laxana Troi, Q

51. Michael Dorn

52. Alexander

53. Prune juice

54. Rick Berman, Ron Moore, Brannon Braga

55. It crashes

56. The International Apparel Mart in Dallas, Texas

57. It defecated on him

58. New York City

59. *Chicago Mobs of the Twenties*

60. Pollux IV

61. Argelius II

62. Archanis IV

63. Medusa

64. Scalos

65. Stratos

66. He is immortal when dwelling in Earth's environment

67. High-energy X-ray lasers

68. John Daily

69. Ben Finney

70. 2267

71. Grups

72. Alexana Devos

73. Historian

74. Harpsichord

75. Anan 7

Level IV: Warp Factor 1

1. Three

2. Three

3. It is used as a private transmitter for personal messages

4. Under no circumstances is the receiver of the code to approach the transmitting planet

5. A laser beacon

6. Morse code

7. Black Jack

8. U.S.S. Republic

9. A dozen

10. The Galactic Cultural Exchange Project

11. Radans

12. It has more power than 10,000 cobalt bombs

13. Metal disk

14. It drew its energy from the life forms it surrounded

15. The Cochrane deceleration maneuver

16. Sympathetic magic

17. Universal translator

18. Plomeek soup

19. I.S.S. Enterprise

20. 4th magnitude

21. Quark, Rom, Nog, Odo

22. Tony Todd, star of the movie *Candyman*

23. Lenara

24. Patrick Stewart

25. Three years

26. Warp 4.7 or faster

27. 1991

28. Robert Egan, a stage director

29. John deLancie (Q)

30. "Mrs. Colombo"

31. 70 light years

32. Left

33. Robert Beltran

34. Kazon

35. Talaxians

36. They live underground

37. Space equipment with godlike power similar to V'Ger

38. Tim Russ

39. Nicholas Locarno

40. *Going to Extremes, Home Front, Second Chance*

41. Kes

42. Human

43. Roxanna Biggs-Dawson

44. Coach Cutlip

45. Kes; *Phenom*

46. Chakotay

47. It can organize and process information like a human brain

48. He heard him recite at a public lecture

49. *The Master and Margarita*

50. Leonard Nimoy

51. Vendikar

52. Claudius Marcus

53. A cigar-shaped space probe called "the planet killer"

54. Security guard Grant

55. His emphasis on cause and motivation rather than dates and events

56. Transporter psychosis

57. 100 years

58. James Doohan

59. Archaeology and anthropology

60. The atavarchron, a temporal portal

61. Gorgan the friendly angel compeled them to do it

62. Victurium

63. Natira

64. Pattern enhancer

65. 50,000 years

66. Lieutenant Mira Romaine

67. Miramanee

68. Holberg 917G

69. Rayna Kapec

70. Governor Cory

Level V: Warp Factor 3

1. Ayelborne, Trefayne, Claymare

2. 1,500 Earth years old

3. Lethe

4. Christopher Thorpe, governor of the Federation Council of the United Federation of Planets

5. 19 years old

6. Several hundred years old

7. Half a million years

8. Vulcan Ambassador to the Federation Council

9. 2020 AD

10. The Fabrini

11. Five lights

12. Orion

13. Hengist

14. 11,000 miles long by almost 3,000 miles wide

15. 240 pounds

16. "Your ship is a garbage scow"

17. Imodene System

18. Gul Madred

19. It is the Vulcan term for "friendship"

20. "Ugly bags of mostly water"

21. Omaha Air Force Base

22. Instrument of Obedience

23. Cerberus

24. A–7

25. Robbiana dermal-optical test

26. The Horta's nest

27. Dark spots in the galaxy

28. Hyronalin

29. Ian

30. Sap

31. It doesn't work

32. Taos Lightning

33. Topaline

34. Glommer

35. Feline supplement 127

36. "Silence"

37. K'Tarans

38. Pasta à la fiarella

39. Joe Piscopo

40. *Mirror Friend, Mirror Foe*

41. b

42. c

43. *The Hunt for Red October*

44. San Francisco Navy Yard

45. They have poison thorns

46. Walter Koenig

47. She is made of pure light

48. Eichner radiation

49. Neural paralyzer

50. Neural scanner

Level VI: Warp Factor 9

1. 387

2. Orange; blue

3. "Elaan of Troyius"

4. Lt. Areel Shaw

5. A martini

6. "Miri"

7. "Tyger, Tyger" and "The Raven"

8. "Beyond Antaries"

9. The salt monster from "The Man Trap"

10. "This Side of Paradise"

11. Dr. Manway

12. #200

13. Three years

14. A hand holding a dove between thumb and forefinger, with a shining sun in the background

15. Psalm 95, Verse 4, "In His hand are the deep places of the Earth"

16. Finagle

17. Dr. Jekyl and Mr. Hyde

18. She is the only person to have turned down a seat on the Federation Council

19. Giant dry worm

20. Tomar

21. Two overlapping ellipses

22. 186,000 miles per second

23. Aucdet IX

24. Planet Q

25. "This Side of Paradise"

26. Mako root

27. Celebium radiation

28. Ryetalyn

29. Virus order 2250 – 67A

30. Kassabe fever

31. *The Primordials*

32. Cordrazine

33. Formazine

34. An engineered microbe that disrupts human genetic material; muon radiation

35. Gamma Quadrant

36. Duonetic field

37. Galamites

38. Her native planet has very low gravity, so her muscles cannot withstand normal Earth gravity

39. Section A–14

40. M5 red dwarf; 40 ships destroyed and 10,000 people killed

41. The Runners

42. 28 years old; 300 years old

43. Baseball

44. Kivas Fajo

45. Bendii Syndrome

46. John Doe

47. The right side

48. Dr. Leah Brahms

49. A race of telepathic historians

50. Dr. Farallon

Level VII: Where No Man Has Gone Before

1. The magnetic field and gravity of the planets disappear

2. Lt. Masters

3. Cestus III

4. The surface of an unnamed asteroid

5. Angela Martine and Robert Tomlinson

6. He questions why war must always be waged when an opponent's weakness is discovered

7. Evans

8. A pink rose

9. Mr. Sulu

10. It was waiting to be asked a question

11. Tools for doing electronics work

12. *Hamlet*

13. His left eye and the entire left side of his head

14. A volatile lubricant

15. Star mapping

16. *TekWars*

17. Commodore Stone

18. Commodore Stone, Captain Chandra, Captain Krasnovsky

19. Dr. Helen Noel

20. Neural Neutralizer

21. More than 50

22. 23rd level

23. Saurian brandy

24. A mind meld with Captain Picard after Picard had mind melded with Sarek

25. They wanted to use it as a base of operations

26. Ayelborne

27. High Commissioner Ferris

28. Latimer

29. M–113

30. Crewman Green

31. Mr. Spock

32. A baffle plate ruptures on a Class J cadet starship he is inspecting

33. Mr. Spock

34. Six days

35. A tricycle

36. A biocomputer and electron microscope

37. Eve, McHuron, Magda, Ruth

38. Double Jack

39. Observing the breakup of a planet

40. By touch, through perspiration

41. Mass insanity

42. The ultra-bright Denevan sun

43. The Archon

44. A lighting panel

45. Birds

46. A tiger

47. "How long?"

48. Adam Nimoy, Leonard Nimoy's son

49. A space displacement reading

50. James Doohan

51. To open diplomatic relationships

52. One to three million annually

53. 45

54. Richard Matheson

Level VIII: To the Galactic Barrier . . . and Beyond

8. He was 29, she was 27

9. The Rigel Colonies

10. Ten

11. Two miles

12. 500

13. Unhappy

14. Intrepid

15. The admission of the planet Coridan to the Federation

16. Sakuro's Disease

17. Tharn

18. Eleven years

19. Zeon

20. Ronald Tracey

21. His communicator

22. Apella

23. 112.37 miles

24. A wheatlike grain

25. Mr. Lurry

26. The Woden, an ore freighter

27. Agamemnon, Hector, Odysseus

28. Kara

29. *TekWars*

30. *Beyond Uhura*

31. Frank Langella

32. $25,000

33. Greg Evigan

34. *Zombies of the Stratosphere*

35. "The Nick of Time"

36. Ted Cassidy (Lurch)

37. Blacula

38. A living spaceship

39. A race of xenophobics erases their memories

40. Tykin's Rift

41. Spock

Level IX: The Voyage Continues

5. Ardana

6. Vanna

7. A false distress signal

8. 400

9. The Klingon Empire

10. Kryton

11. Dr. Ozaba

12. Lal and Thann

13. Three

14. A centurion

15. Xenopolycythemia

16. Larry Marvick

17. Pity

18. A Federation shuttlecraft

19. Bele

20. New equipment

21. Four (dead people on Memory Alpha, return of storm to Memory Alpha, Scotty's death, her own near death)

22. To prevent contamination from violence

23. Spock

24. Amerind

25. Eight times the speed of light

26. By eating food native to the planet

27. 2,300 years old

28. Paul Robeson

29. Holberg 917G

30. To observe and learn about good and evil

31. A boomerang

32. Swahili

33. The Clantons

34. 24 hours

35. A communicator

36. They had no physical affect on the landscape

37. The U.S.S. Defiant

38. He went temporarily insane

39. Loskene

40. "Find the surgeon NOW"

41. Dr. Coleman

42. The Aurora

43. Fifteen

44. Accelerated metabolisms gave them super speed

45. Leonard Nimoy's daughter

46. Genevieve Bujold

47. *Models, Inc.*

48. *All My Children*

49. Patrick Stewart

50. To prevent leg chafing

Level X: '60s Flashback

1. The Paradise Syndrom—2½ months

2. A mint julep

3. Tranya

4. *Alice in Wonderland*

5. "Errand of Mercy"

6. Gertrude

7. The River Lethe, a mythological "River of Forgetfulness"

8. Atru

9. Vulcan lyrette

10. "Molly Malone"

11. Jim Boy

12. Love

13. Language

14. "Plato's Stepchildren"

15. *Tombstone Epitaph*

16. His military victory at Axanar

17. Dr. McCoy

18. Intra-ship transporting

19. "I, Mudd"

20. "Catspaw"

21. Two full stripes

22. Two full stripes and one broken stripe

23. Vulcan lyrette

24. The Jeffrey's Tube

25. Command Intelligence Primary Visual Display

26. The destruction of a previously designated planet

27. It disintegrates

28. Invasion status

29. Two flashes for a no, one flash for a yes

30. War

31. A planet with conditions similar to Earth

32. Starfleet Academy

33. Starfleet Command

34. With a tractor beam

35. The captain must make a notation in his log and initiate an investigation

36. General Order #7

37. Klingon side arms

38. Thirty seconds

39. A bureaucrat or stuffed shirt

40. Irillium

41. 643 miles, 2021 feet, 2.04 inches

42. Zenite

43. Yellow, green, pink

44. The Fifth Interstellar Geophysical Conference

45. Mr. Scott: Queen to Queen's Level
    Kirk: Queen to King's Level I

46. The transmuter

47. A Kligat

48. An enormous artificial sphere enclosing a star

49. Giant ell-birds

50. An agonizer

51. Harcourt Fenton Mudd

52. A seven-foot-tall bipedal lizard creature

53. Dr. Brown

54. Reger and Marplon

55. Because they are not "part of the body"

56. Lenore Karidian

57. Particle Fountain

58. Rodent

59. Thirty

60. The Keeper

61. A barillium titanium alloy covered by a self-renewing plastic skin

62. Koloth

63. Orion

64. The Hill People

65. The Providers

66. Via fission

67. Parmen

68. Green

69. They both have the last name Grayson

70. Yarnek, a rock creature

71. Camus II

72. They rescued endangered cultures from catastrophes and relocated them to safe planets

73. Kollos

74. Morgs and Eymorgs

75. Galt

76. Odona

77. Hodin

78. Earth probe Nomad and alien probe Tan Ru

79. Farrell

80. Antennae

81. Lithium cracking

82. Petri

83. Daedalus

84. Cygnet 14

85. Borgia plant

86. Deneva

87. Exo III

88. Starbase 11

89. Mining pergium

90. Colony Beta 6

91. Sybo

92. Theragen

93. Vina

94. Mining

95. Tellun System

96. Earth outposts 2, 3, 4

97. Planet Q

98. Omicron Delta Region

99. Benecia Colony

100. 1150

Bonus Level: Shore Leave

1. Mark Lenard

2. William Shatner

3. He kidnaps the entire Enterprise crew

4. William Shatner

5. Sean Connery

6. Mark Lenard

7. "You will be remembered with honor."

8. HIjol ("beam me aboard") or jul ylchu' ("activate transporter beam")

9. John Vornholt

10. *Power Hungry*

11. It is a computer program that takes control of the Enterprise-D

12. *Gulliver's Fugitives*

13. K'vin

14. *Nightshade*

15. Principles and rules of business success; 285

16. Gint

17. Family and friendship

18. Opportunity + Instinct = Profit

19. "Anything worth doing is worth doing for money"

20. "Keep your lies consistent"

21. Huyperian beetle

22. "Dignity and an empty sack is worth the sack"

23. oo-mox

24. Garak

25. They buy and sell them for a profit

26. Kim Cattrall

27. James Doohan

28. Iman

29. "Row, Row, Row Your Boat"

30. *A Tale of Two Cities*

31. Persis Khambatta

32. Omega Cygni

33. John Larroquette

34. Pagh; Kargan

35. It's an ocean planet

36. Sonak

37. Sonic disruptor field

38. A medical device that prevents patients from depleting their body's blood supply

39. Galvan

40. Kesla

41. A giant space amoeba

42. American Continental Institutes

43. Nick Ramus

44. First Federation

45. The natives are cannibals who will eat their own species as well as others

46. Zeons

47. $44 million

48. Majet Barrett

49. Nancy Parsons

50. Michelle Phillips

51. The Chiokis Starship Construction Company. 2211 AD

52. 0.785 second

53. 503.1 feet

54. Workbee

55. Twenty

56. Cyanide in the plant's cellulose structure

57. Qo'noS. Other acceptable answers: Klinzhai, YuQ

58. A long ceremonial Klingon sword

59. Kahless the Unforgettable

60. Zentaurs (they boil the haunch into a soup)

61. Gene Roddenberry

62. Karin Blair

63. Leonard Nimoy

64. On a sheep farm outside of Aberdeen, Scotland

65. Hawaii

66. Irina Galilulan

67. Nurse Christine Chapel

68. It wiped her mind clean.

69. He was a Starfleet engineer stationed aboard the starship U.S.S. Yorktown

70. A Vulcan ritual of passage into manhood

71. George and Martha Kirk

72. Strategic and tactical skills

73. Iron weaving; playing the flute

74. Rogo Danar

75. Avery Brooks

76. Roana

77. Mullibok

78. Nichelle Nichols

79. San Francisco

80. Seven hundred years old

81. Khitomer

82. A xenozooligist in the Modine System

83. Deanna Troi

84. U.S.S. Tripoli

85. Kyle and Elizabeth Riker

86. July 13, 2005 in Labarre, France

87. Martian Utopia Planetia Shipyards

88. The shakaar

89. Aldeberan Musical Academy

90. Ivernia II

91. Prewarp engines, especially impulse thruster configurations

92. Odo

93. Vulcan and Romulan

94. Chancellor Gorkon; Pink

95. They put presents in a gift box that has a humanoid face on it and greets the recipient of the present with a message.

96. Miradorns

97. It is the Klingon term for sex.

98. EPI capacitor

99. Tachyon detection grid

100. 1 Latinum

Appendix A

Star Trek Vendors

Companies that sell *Star Trek* publications, collectibles, and memorabilia

New Eye Studio
P.O. Box 632
Willimantic, CT 06226
Star Trek *action figures and other items*

Figures
P.O. Box 19482
Johnston, RI 02919
Collectible toys and action figures of Star Trek *and other science fiction characters*

Franklin Mint
Franklin Center, PA 19091–0001
Star Trek *collectibles*

FXM
P.O. Box 186
Keyport, NJ 07735
phone 908–583–8373
Star Trek *model kits*

GSM
Box 325
Rosyln, NY 11576
phone 800–336–5900
Next Generation *commemorative postage stamps*

The Hamilton Collection
4810 Executive Park Ct.
P.O. Box 44051
Jacksonville, FL 32231–4051
Models, plaques, and other collectibles

John F. Green Inc.
1821 W. Jacaranda
Fullerton, CA 92633
phone 714–526–5467 or 800–807–4759
Plastic model kits

Martin Enterprises
P.O. Box 12211
Burke, VA 22009–2211
Star Trek *videos including bloopers, original episodes, animated series, and movies*

Starlog Group
475 Park Avenue South
New York, NY 10016
phone 800-STARLOG
Cards, magazines, posters, film cells, action figures, T-shirts, drawings, autographs, and other collectibles

Lightspeed Enterprises
P.O. Box 75
New York, NY 10276
Latex masks, costumes, and make-up for Trekkers who want to dress up as their favorite Star Trek *characters*

S&P Parker's Movie Market
P.O. Box 1868
Laguna Beach, CA 92652
phone 714–376–0326
Photos of Star Trek *and other movie and TV stars*

Script City
8033 Sunset Blvd.
#1500
Hollywood, CA 90046
phone 213–871–0707
Thousands of movie and TV scripts, including Star
Trek

Star Tech
P.O. Box 456
Dunlap, TN 37327
Star Trek collectibles: books, plates, scripts, posters,
models, *tapes, blueprints, and more*

800-TREKKER
P.O. Box 13131
Reading, PA 19612–3131
phone 800–873–5537
Catalog of collectibles from Star Trek *and other science fiction TV shows. My favorite item: A TV remote
control that looks like a phaser.*

VR Audio
7051 Highway 70 South
Nashville, TN 37221
*Offers a CD that duplicates the sounds aboard the
Enterprise's bridge.*

Wireless Music & Audio Collection
Minnesota Public Radio
P.O. Box 64454
St. Paul, MN 55164–0454
1–800–733–3369
*Catalog of audio cassettes, software, CDs, and CD
ROMs. Contains many items from popular TV shows
and films including* Star Trek.

Appendix B

Magazines, Fanzines

Bewilderbeast
Dennis Fischer
6820 E. Alondra
Paramount, CA 90723

Dusty Jones
1009 East-West Highway
Takoma Park, MD 20912

Enterprise Incidents
James Van Hise
P.O. Box 2546
Yucca Valley, CA 92286–2546
Various back issues available.

Garden Spot
Bill Hupe
916 Lamp Road
Mason, MI 48854–9554

McCoy's Toy
Bonnie Guyan
323 Fordhook Avenue
Johnstown, PA 15905

Newsletter at the End of the Universe
Boston Star Trek Association
P.O. Box 1108
Boston, MA 02103

Our Favorite Things
Elan Press
P.O. Box 615
Macedon, NY 14502–0615

Starfleet Communique
P.O. Box 430
Burnsville, NC 28714

Star Trek Deep Space Nine Magazine
475 Park Avenue South
New York, NY 10016

To Boldly Go
Starlite Press
P.O. Box 2455
Dabville, CA 94526

Trekzine Times
Forever Productions
P.O. Box 75
New York, NY 10276
True Vulcan Professions

Warped Factor
T'Khutian Press
200 E. Thomas Street
Lansing, MI 48909

Star Trek Voyager Magazine
475 Park Avenue South
New York, NY 10016

Yeoman Press
5465 Vallas Avenue
Bronx, NY 10471

Appendix C

Star Trek Events

Creation
411 N. Central Avenue, Suite 300
Glendale, CA 91203
phone 818–409–0960
Major producer of Star Trek *conventions and shows nationwide.*

Cruise Trek
P.O. Box 2038
Agoura Hills, CA 01376–2038
phone 818–597–2940
Cruises with Star Trek *themes with cast members on board*

Bibliography

Alexander, David. *Star Trek Creator: The Authorized Biography of Gene Roddenberry* (New York: ROC Books, 1994).

Asherman, Allan. *The Star Trek Compendium* (New York: Pocket Books, 1993).

Asherman, Allan. *The Star Trek Interview Book* (New York: Pocket Books, 1988).

Behr, Ira. *The Ferengi Rules of Acquisition* (New York: Pocket Books, 1995).

Bly, Robert W. *The Ultimate Unauthorized Star Trek Quiz Book* (New York: HarperCollins, 1994).

Farrand, Phil. *The Nitpicker's Guide for Next Generation Trekkers* (New York: Dell, 1993).

Gross, Edward and Mark Altman. *Captain's Log: The Complete Trek Voyages* (New York: Image Publishing, 1993).

Gross, Edward (ed.). *The Making of the Trek Films* (New York: Image Publishing, 1994).

Johnson, Shane. *Star Trek: Mr. Scott's Guide to the Enterprise* (New York: Pocket Books, 1987).

Krauss, Lawrence M. *The Physics of Star Trek* (New York: HarperCollins, 1994).

Nemecek, Larry. *The Star Trek: The Next Generation Companion* (New York: Pocket Books, 1992).

Okrand, Marc. *The Official Guide to Klingon Words and Phrases* (New York: Pocket Books, 1992).

Okuda, Michael and Denise Okuda. *Star Trek Chronology: The History of the Future* (New York: Pocket Books, 1993).

Okuda, Michael, Denise Okuda, and Debbie Mirek. *The Star Trek Encyclopedia: A Reference Guide to the Future* (New York: Pocket Books, 1994).

Peel, John. *The Trek Encyclopedia: Second Edition* (Las Vegas: Pioneer, 1993).

Reeves-Stevens, Judith and Garfield Reeves-Stevens. *The Making of Star Trek Deep Space Nine* (New York: Pocket Books, 1994).

Shatner, William with Chris Kreski. *Star Trek Memories* (New York: HarperCollins, 1993).

Shatner, William with Chris Kreski. *Star Trek Movie Memories* (New York: HarperCollins, 1994).

Schuster, Hal and Wendy Rathbone. *Trek: The Unauthorized A–Z* (New York: HarperCollins, 1994).

Takei, George. *To the Stars: The Autobiography of George Takei* (New York: Pocket Books, 1994).

Van Hise, James. *The Best of Enterprise Incidents: The Magazine for Star Trek Fans* (Las Vegas: Pioneer Books).

Van Hise, James. *The Classic Trek Crew Book* (Las Vegas: Pioneer Books, 1993).

Van Hise, James and Hal Schuster. *Let's Trek: The Budget Traveller's Guide to Klingon Worlds* (Las Vegas: Pioneer Books, 1994).

Van Hise, James. *The Man Who Created Star Trek: Gene Roddenberry* (Las Vegas: Pioneer Books, 1992).

Van Hise, James. *The Special Effects of Star Trek* (Las Vegas: Pioneer Books, 1993).

Van Hise, James. *Trek: The Next Generation Crew Book* (Las Vegas: Pioneer Books, 1993).

Van Hise, James. *Trek vs. The Next Generation* (Las Vegas: Pioneer Books, 1993).

Van Hise, James. *Trek: The Printed Adventure* (Las Vegas: Pioneer Books, 1993).

Van Hise, James. *The Unauthorized Trek: Deep Space: The Voyage Continues* (Las Vegas: Pioneer Books, 1994).

Van Hise, James. *The Voyage Continues . . . Trek: The Next Generation: Second Edition* (Las Vegas: Pioneer Books, 1992).

Van Hise, James, and Hal Schuster. *Trek Crew Companion* (Las Vegas: Pioneer Books, 1994).

About the Author

Robert W. Bly has been a science fiction and comic book fan for more than 30 years. He is the author of more than 30 books including *Creative Careers: Real Jobs in Glamour Fields* (John Wiley & Sons) and *The Ultimate Unauthorized Star Trek Quiz Book* (HarperCollins). His articles have appeared in such publications as *Writer's Digest, Amtrak Express, Cosmopolitan, City Paper, Science Books & Films,* and *New Jersey Monthly.*

A chemical engineer by training, Mr. Bly is a full-time freelance writer working for such clients as IBM, AT&T, AlliedSignal, CoreStates Financial Corporation, Swiss Bank, and EBI Medical Systems. He lives in New Milford, NJ with his wife Amy and sons Alex and Stephen.